Hearst Castle

The Official Pictorial Guide

by Nancy E. Loe

Published under license from Hearst San Simeon State Historical Monument.
"Hearst Castle," "Hearst Monument," "La Cuesta Encantada," and "The Enchanted Hill"
are trademarks and service marks of Hearst San Simeon State Historical Monument.

Produced by Companion Press
Bishop, California

Edited by Jane Freeburg
Designed by Lucy Brown
Printed in Hong Kong
through Bolton Associates,
San Rafael, California

ISBN 0-944197-14-0

Tenth printing, 2004

Acknowledgments

My thanks to Deborah Weldon, regional director of DPR's San Simeon Region, who strongly supports the accurate interpretation of Hearst Castle. Her confidence in me is greatly appreciated. San Simeon's chief curator, Sandra Barghini, made this project a success. Members of her staff, including curator Hoyt Fields, historian Robert Pavlik, photographer John Blades, and registrar Natalie Sylvester came to my aid throughout this enterprise. My thanks as well to David Walch, Dean of Library Services at Cal Poly, who actively encourages professional accomplishment, and to Joan Kennedy of Special Collections for her timely assistance with the Morgan Collection. NL

Illustration Credits

Contents

Chapter One

Building On "The Enchanted Hill"

William Randolph Hearst gave the romantic name of *La Cuesta Encantada* to his vast and palatial California estate soon after construction began in 1919. Situated on a crest of the Santa Lucia mountains overlooking the Pacific Ocean, "The Enchanted Hill" today covers 137 acres, capped by four impressive residences created by architect Julia Morgan for her well-known client.

Popularly known as either San Simeon or Hearst Castle, the estate is now a California historical monument and an international attraction, drawing nearly one million visitors each year. Curators and other professionals tend the many art and architectural collections that the late publisher compulsively purchased throughout his long and vigorous life.

William Randolph Hearst was born on April 29, 1863, in San Francisco. The only child of George and Phoebe Apperson Hearst, young Willie was considered precocious by his mother, who encouraged his early appreciation of the fine arts. His father offered an intriguing contrast, for he was a self-made man whose first fortune was

discovered in the silver mines of the Comstock Lode in 1859.

George Hearst continued to roam the western states, doubling and redoubling his holdings in mines and real estate. By 1865, George began to acquire large parcels of land throughout the West. Among his first purchases were the original Mexican ranchos of *Piedra Blanca*, *San Simeon*, and *Santa Rosa*, portions of which were bought for as little as seventy cents an acre.

The family's increasing wealth allowed ten-year-old Willie Hearst and his mother to make a Grand Tour of Europe for eighteen months. Hearst's fondness for art collecting began on this trip, and continued to be a fascinating and ultimately indispensable part of his adult life. Phoebe Hearst encouraged this fondness with the purchase of a marble wellhead from Verona that still graces the south terrace at San Simeon today.

Will Hearst enrolled at Harvard College in 1882. He served as the business manager of the college's humor magazine, where he was "first introduced to the drug of printer's ink," in the dramatic words of *Time* magazine. During his college years, Hearst also displayed great interest in entertainment, theatre, and dramatics,

Construction on "The Enchanted Hill." With guest houses ready for occupancy, architect Julia Morgan began work on Casa Grande, *seen here at the extreme left, in 1926. (Inset) Detail of tile designed by Julia Morgan.*

Mr Hearst thinks there should be some thing here

This preliminary sketch of the main entrance to Casa Grande was submitted to Hearst in 1926.

Phoebe Hearst with her daughter-in-law Millicent, and her grandchildren George, William Jr., and John.

At the time work on the San Simeon estate began, Hearst was 56 years old and Morgan was 47. Their close collaboration spanned 27 years.

despite his shy nature. Unfortunately, young Will did not devote as much time to his formal studies as he did to the *Harvard Lampoon* and the Hasty Pudding Club, and so was asked to leave in his junior year.

Hearst plunged into journalism at the age of 23, editing the foundering San Francisco *Examiner*, a Democratic newspaper his father owned. Hearst poured prodigious amounts of his time and George's money into the *Examiner*, using the sensational techniques for reporting the news pioneered by New York publisher Joseph Pulitzer. Hearst possessed enormous energy, expansive imagination, and a bankroll that must have seemed limitless to his rivals in the publishing business.

Emboldened, Hearst went on to purchase or begin papers in New York, Chicago, Seattle, Los Angeles, Boston, and other American cities, replicating his San Francisco strategies and successes. He further enlarged upon his publishing empire by buying or founding national magazines such as *Motor, Connoisseur, Good Housekeeping, Cosmopolitan,* and *Popular Mechanics.* By the turn of the century, Hearst's papers and magazines were a great success and his reputation for boldness was widely recognized. In 1913, his journalism

empire thriving, Hearst expanded into the production of newsreels. By the early–1920s, Hearst had formed Cosmopolitan Productions in New York City to make newsreels, serials and feature films. Cosmopolitan moved to California in 1924, where Hearst forged an alliance with Louis B. Mayer at Metro-Goldwyn-Mayer that would last until 1935.

Hearst married on the eve of his fortieth birthday, choosing Millicent Willson, a New York entertainer, as his bride. They had five sons: George; William Randolph, Jr.; John; and twin boys, Randolph and David. The family lived a good part of the year in New York, but made frequent trips to the

An early aerial view of "The Enchanted Hill," showing Casa Grande's first towers. Hearst decided to raze the original towers for a larger design that included a carillon.

San Simeon ranch, which had grown to be Hearst's favorite of all the family's holdings.

Hearst considered these to be camping trips, even though he and Millicent, their sons and the domestic help retired at night to elaborate tents. Pitched upon wooden flooring, each of these canvas shelters contained partitions for four rooms. Separate tents were erected for dining, sleeping, and storage. This tent village was grouped around "a great circus tent with board flooring covered with soft, warm rugs rich as those of a Bedouin chieftain's," according to his principal biographer, W.A. Swanberg. Trips to California also meant stops at his mother's ranch near Pleasanton, where the children often stayed for longer visits.

Now widowed, Phoebe Apperson Hearst devoted her time equally to travelling and distributing largesse from her late husband's considerable fortune. Her philanthropies were numerous, and included preserving redwood trees in California, restoring Mount Vernon in Virginia, beginning kindergarten education in Washington, D.C., building public libraries in western mining communities, and endowing numerous academic endeavors at the University of California at Berkeley. It was here that Phoebe met Julia Morgan, a subdued but determined student who wished to be an architect.

Julia Morgan was born in San Francisco on January 20, 1872, and raised in Oakland, California. As the first step toward her professional goal, Morgan obtained a civil engineering degree from Berkeley in 1894. Because there were no California schools teaching architecture at that time, Morgan travelled to Paris to study at the *École Nationale et Spéciale des Beaux-Arts*, upon the advice of her mentor, architect Bernard Maybeck.

Although she arrived in Paris to begin her studies in 1896, Morgan was refused admission for two years because the *École des Beaux-Arts* had never conceived of allowing women to study at the institution. Discouraged when she failed several entrance examinations, she persevered when she learned that professors had deliberately failed her so that "young girls would not be encouraged" to study or practice architecture. Morgan was eventually admitted in November of 1898 and advanced to the top class within a year, a feat no other student had accomplished. In 1902 she became the first woman and one of the few Americans to receive *École des Beaux-Arts* certification in architecture.

Upon her return to San Francisco, Morgan secured a position in the offices of architect John Galen Howard. Howard had opened an office in Berkeley after he had won the Phoebe Apperson Hearst Architectural Competition to design a master building plan for the University of California. Morgan drew the elevations and designed the decorative details for the Mining Building, a commission from Phoebe Hearst in memory of her mining magnate husband, George.

By 1904 Morgan had opened her own office. Phoebe Hearst retained her services to complete an elaborate *hacienda* for her Pleasanton ranch. Morgan also began to add institutional work to her already large number of private residence commissions. Her institutional work was often commissioned by women's institutions, such as schools, colleges, sororities, and social and community clubs. The national board of the YWCA asked her to serve as their principal architect in New York City. Morgan declined the offer, but

Morgan and her staff made thousands of detailed drawings for San Simeon. Her classical training at the École des Beaux-Arts is evident in the drawing of an "A" House interior (above) and a tiled floor design (right).

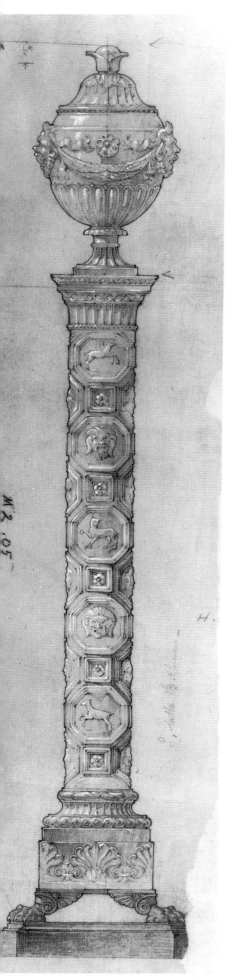

This marble lamp standard, changed slightly from the Morgan drawing seen here, was placed on the main terrace.

These marble lions await placement in the fountain on lower "C" Terrace.

designed YWCAs in California, Utah, and Hawaii.

In 1919 Julia Morgan was commissioned by William Randolph Hearst to design a main building and guest houses on the San Simeon ranch. Phoebe Hearst had died that spring in the worldwide influenza epidemic, and Hearst had inherited San Simeon (now a ranch of many thousands of acres), additional real estate, his mother's art and book collections, and an estimated $11 million in cash.

At the time that San Simeon was begun, Hearst was 56 years old and Morgan was 47. She had been practicing architecture for nearly twenty years and had at least 450 commissions to her credit. Morgan's classical training at the *École des Beaux-Arts,* together with her knowledge of engineering and her considerable experience using reinforced concrete, made her ideally suited to the enormous tasks Hearst proposed. Given her already thriving architectural practice, Morgan usually travelled to San Simeon on Friday evenings and worked there through the weekend before returning to San Francisco.

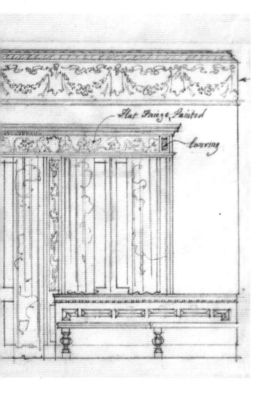

Flat frieze, Painted

carving

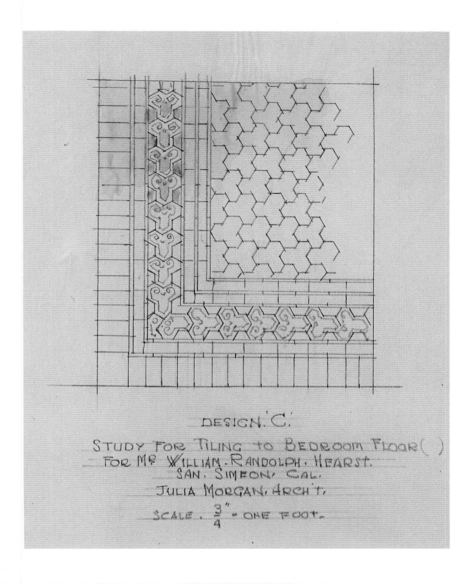

DESIGN "C".

STUDY FOR TILING TO BEDROOM FLOOR ( )
FOR MR WILLIAM.RANDOLPH.HEARST.
SAN.SIMEON, CAL.
JULIA MORGAN, ARCH'T.

SCALE. $\frac{3}{4}$" = ONE FOOT.

Two hermae, *or Roman busts, were shipped from London to San Simeon in 1921. Morgan wrote to Hearst suggesting that they be placed "as decoration in the court of house A."*

Three guest houses and a central structure, *Casa Grande*, were designed after much deliberation between architect and client. Hearst wrote to Morgan that he "wished for something a little different from what other people are doing in California," which ultimately led to the unique and harmonious blend of styles and periods that is San Simeon. Hearst initially lived in "A" House or *Casa del Mar*, the first of the guest houses to be completed. Guest houses "B" (*Casa del Monte)* and "C" (*Casa del Sol*) were followed by *Casa Grande*.

The main house has approximately 115 rooms on four floors and nearly 45,000 square feet of space. Morgan's design amply provided for Hearst's *Casa Grande* guests with 26 bedrooms, 32 bathrooms, 14 sitting rooms, two libraries, a dining room measuring 2,000 square feet, 30 fireplaces, a billiard room, a beauty salon, and a movie theater with projection room. In addition, the service wing of the main house contains a pantry, servants' dining room, kitchen, 12 bedrooms, 10 bathrooms, and seven other rooms used by domestic staff. The 9,000 square foot basement contains nine vaults, a wine cellar, a boiler room and walk-in coolers. The switchboard and telegraph office were located in the construction foreman's office. In addition to the San Simeon estate that exists today, Hearst and Morgan also had unrealized plans for a bowling alley, ballroom, banquet hall, art gallery, clock tower, polo field, topiary maze, and two more guest houses.

Morgan completed indoor and outdoor swimming pools, tennis courts, a mile-and-a-half pergola, a reservoir, greenhouses, animal shelters for a growing menagerie, barracks for the construction workers, plus five warehouses and a small village of houses for permanent staff on San Simeon Bay. She coped with the difficult task of getting construction materials, as well as art, up the steep Santa Lucia hillsides, using chain-driven trucks and teams of horses. Morgan, her staff, and the construction workers also contended with capricious weather as well as spontaneous visits from Hearst himself.

In February of 1927, he decided to come to San Simeon with a party of guests. A series of severe rainstorms also visited the hilltop. After the first storm, Hearst personally wrote a letter to Morgan saying, "We had a lively time in house A last night. The storm was severe and I spent most of the night ripping off the weather stripping in my room. The darn stuff sounded like a flock of saxophones going at full tilt in a jazz band."

The next day a second letter from Hearst arrived, suggesting that the doors to "A" House be made "water and

Typical of Morgan's attention to detail are the tile designs above and at right.

draft proof with metal weather strips. If antique iron doors [do] not permit this, don't use antique iron. Let's have COMFORT AND HEALTH before so much art. The art won't do us any good if we are all dead of pneumonia." Further rainstorms prompted this pithy letter to the construction foreman:

We are all leaving the hill. We are drowned, blown and frozen out. . . . Before we build anything more let's make what we have built practical, comfortable and beautiful. If we can't do that we might just as well change the names of the houses to Pneumonia House, Diphtheria House and Influenza Bungalow. The main house we can call the Clinic. I am not coming back to the hill until we put the small houses on a liveable basis. . . . The weather strips wail like a chorus of lost souls, the windows leak

The western exposure of "A" House, overlooking the sea.

little rivers of running water and under the doors the cold draughts blow like . . . hurricanes until the rugs flop on the floor. . . All who could have left and the few who remain are eagerly waiting a chance to get out.

Despite his threat, Hearst remained on the hilltop. That weekend, Morgan made her customary trip to the building site where they considered various methods of weatherproofing the buildings. Hearst's pique eventually subsided along with the winter storms.

Thousands of blueprints and architectural drawings exist for San Simeon; many of them bear Hearst's handwritten opinions of Morgan's work as well as requests for changes and improvements. Hearst's ideas for San Simeon were so fluid that he sometimes requested changes even after the work had been successfully completed.

The Neptune Pool, perhaps the most splendid outdoor pool Morgan designed, took twelve years to perfect. When construction began in this area in 1924, Hearst asked for a landscaped garden with a small ornamental pool. Two years later, as work neared completion on the "Temple Gardens," Hearst requested a much larger pool, suitable for swimming, and the addition of a cascade to the design. Morgan designed a new pool; the renovation was completed in 1926 – 1927. In 1934, Hearst asked Morgan to enlarge the pool once again to accommodate the present Greek temple facade, a larger cascade, and additional statue-filled alcoves.

Examples of other changes to finished work abound. The Celestial Suites in the twin towers of Casa Grande were added when Hearst ordered the original towers redesigned and enlarged to include a carillon. The addition of two wings to the rear of *Casa Grande* disturbed the view from the Doge's Suite, so Hearst asked that the room's fireplace (and flue) be moved and exchanged with the offending window.

Morgan accepted these and other changes from her unpredictable client with her characteristic calm, drew new plans, and billed Hearst for the changes. Although Hearst sometimes chaffed at delays, there is no record that Morgan ever responded in kind, an astonishing feat for a working relationship that lasted twenty-seven years.

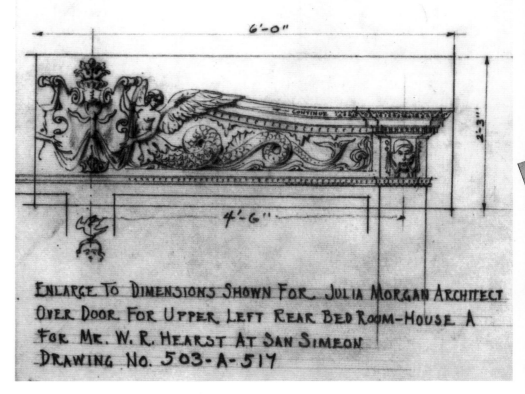

ENLARGE TO DIMENSIONS SHOWN FOR JULIA MORGAN ARCHITECT OVER DOOR FOR UPPER LEFT REAR BED ROOM-HOUSE A FOR MR. W. R. HEARST AT SAN SIMEON DRAWING No. 503-A-517

Crafts workers on Morgan's staff at San Simeon completed detailed design elements under her direction.

Terra cotta oil jars from Sicily, large enough to hold this whimsical construction worker, add Mediterranean touches to the grounds at San Simeon.

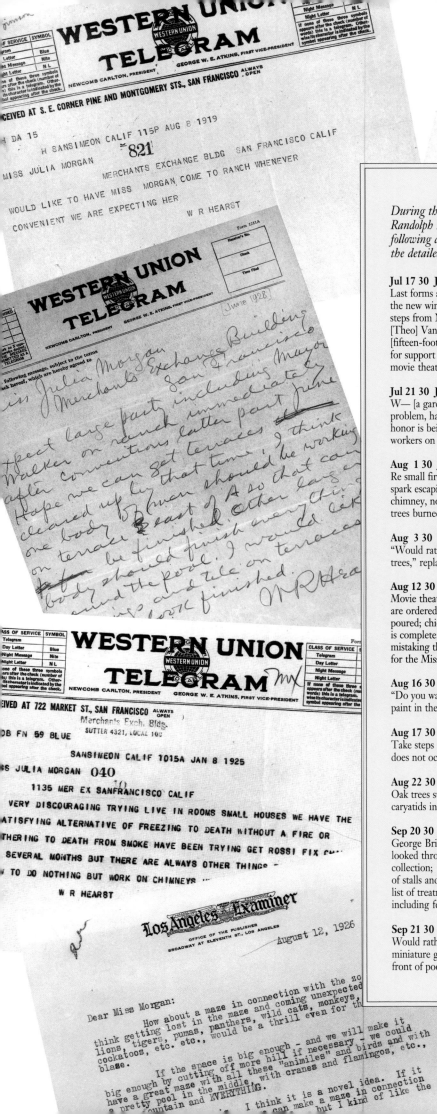

Attention to Detail

During the construction of San Simeon, architect Julia Morgan and client William Randolph Hearst consulted with each other frequently by mail and telegram. The following digest of their correspondence from July to December of 1930 is typical of the detailed correspondence between them.

Jul 17 30 JM to WRH
Last forms are being taken down from the new wing towers; ready to pour the steps from North Terrace to Esplanade; [Theo] Van der Loo is casting caryatids [fifteen-foot draped female figures used for support and decoration of walls in movie theatre]

Jul 21 30 JM to WRH
W— [a gardener] seems to have a mental problem, has been acting queer; feels his honor is being damaged by other workers on the hill

Aug 1 30 JM to WRH
Re small fire on the hill, caused by a spark escaping from wire mesh guard on chimney, no structural damage, but a few trees burned

Aug 3 30 WRH to JM
"Would rather have buildings burn than trees," replant immediately

Aug 12 30 JM to WRH
Movie theatre carpet and chair coverings are ordered; concrete for caryatids poured; chicken farm construction work is complete; "Many tourists are mistaking the new buildings [at Jolon] for the Mission [San Antonio]"

Aug 16 30 JM to WRH
"Do you want gold leafing or gold gilt paint in theater?"

Aug 17 30 WRH to JM
Take steps to insure that another fire does not occur

Aug 22 30 JM to WRH
Oak trees survived the fire pretty well; caryatids installed in theater

Sep 20 30 JM to WRH
George Brittany, zoological consultant, looked through the entire animal collection; recommends regular cleaning of stalls and shelters; enclosed detailed list of treatment for each specific animal, including feeding instructions

Sep 21 30 WRH to JM
Would rather have indoor pool than miniature golf; also wants large lawn in front of pool for croquet

Oct 1 30 WRH to JM
"Please have the tennis court remain painted grey" because the green paint comes off on the tennis balls

Oct 6 30 WRH to JM
Please suspend all building operations until May 1

Oct 10 30 WRH to JM
Finish various projects, and close camp on November 1

Oct 25 30 WRH to JM
Need a thoroughly competent head gardener, please review candidates

Oct 27 30 WRH to JM
Nigel Keep [a gardener] wants a new house in the village and should have one

Nov 1 30 JM to WRH
Hiring new gardener, going over former ones that were on the hill

Dec 3 30 JM to WRH
All construction expenses on hill eliminated, except for people working on mosaic for the indoor pool

Dec 15 30 WRH to JM
Please proceed with music room, theatre and projection booth

Dec 16 30 JM to WRH
Please begin building animal shelters after the holidays

Dec 17 30 WRH to JM
Please finish tower rooms. "I find W— interjecting himself into work which is out of his department . . ."

Dec 18 30 JM to WRH
"Will be down tomorrow and arrange for things you ask"

Dec 20 30 WRH to JM
Add lights in the breakfast room, curtains in Gothic sitting room

Dec 29 30 WRH to JM
Please put eight ladders in the indoor pool instead of four

All letters from the Julia Morgan Collection courtesy of Special Collections Department, Robert E. Kennedy Library, California Polytechnic State University.

Chapter Two
Hearst The Collector

 Julia Morgan conferred with William Randolph Hearst not only on the architectural design of each structure, but also on the placement of the antiques and works of art purchased for San Simeon. The massive construction site inspired this already avid collector to new heights. The International Studio Art Corporation was formed in New York, as a subsidiary of the Hearst Corporation, to cope with the flood of purchases. Staff members there arranged for the transportation of art and architectural elements by rail or by ship to west coast ports. Further arrangements were needed to transport the contents by steamer to San Simeon Bay. Morgan's workers reinforced the original wharf George Hearst had built on the bay, adding a railroad siding so that shipments could be unloaded easily and rolled to the warehouses she had designed. Here members of her staff worked to inventory and record his many purchases.

Eventually some of these architectural elements and art objects were used at San Simeon or other Hearst estates. Some were sent to Hollywood for use on movie sets or to other cities for loan to museums. Still other shipments were never uncrated. By 1930, the five warehouses at San Simeon were full and even Hearst's Bronx warehouse was nearing its entire city block capacity.

W.R. Hearst, like many other wealthy collectors of his day, was able to indulge in his enthusiasm for art and art collecting with virtually no restraints. The collections formed by Andrew Mellon, the Rockefeller family, Isabella Stewart Gardner, the Vanderbilt family and J.P. Morgan rival the quality, if not the quantity, of Hearst's collections. Nearly all of these notable nineteenth-century American collectors had several motives. Styling their homes after Old World villas and decorating them with European art conferred status upon the newly wealthy, required large sums of discretionary income, and displayed their taste and discernment. In typical Hearst fashion, Hearst embraced these hallmarks of his peers and added several of his own.

He requested that Morgan incorporate his collections into the function as well as the form of the residence. Most of his peers displayed important pieces in their homes or donated *objets* to public museums. However, W.R. Hearst had not only San Simeon as his

Julia Morgan designed this library on the second floor of Casa Grande *for Hearst's guests. His splendid collection of Greek vases, displayed along the walls, are secured in the event of earthquakes. (Inset) Mermaids grace a tile border designed by Morgan.*

The four statues of Sekhmet, the lion-faced Egyptian goddess of war and battle, are the oldest works of art at San Simeon, dating from 1350-1200 B.C. Hearst acquired the pieces in 1935; Morgan designed the Egyptian-inspired tile risers and selected the location.

display case, but also Wyntoon, an even larger estate on the McCloud River in northern California; a triplex in Manhattan; a million-acre ranch in Mexico; a fourteenth-century castle in Wales; a 100-room "beach house" in Santa Monica; and several houses in Beverly Hills. Now separated from his wife, Hearst spent more time in California, while his wife Millicent maintained a luxury flat in Manhattan and her Long Island estate at Sands Point. All of these houses inspired the collector in Hearst, who rapidly filled them with even more treasures.

The sheer volume of Hearst's purchases indicates his compulsion to collect. Art dealers were astounded,

notes Hearst biographer William Swanberg, "by the promiscuity of his buying. Most collectors specialized, but he was interested in everything from *howdahs* to reliquaries, and he seemed gripped by an uncontrollable urge to buy, buy, buy."

Hearst bought art for its impact upon the viewer. According to art historian Patricia Failing, ". . . from Hearst's point of view, museum-quality status was obviously not a prime concern. Impact and impression were his most evident goals in decorating; if the desired effect was achieved, breath-taking juxtapositions of quality. . . were entirely justified." The nucleus of several of his extraordinary collections

were bequeathed to him by his mother. Hearst's additional purchases were based not only on dealers' recommendations, but also on his own knowledge of the field. He bought through most of the well-known auction houses in London and New York, including Sotheby's, Joseph Duveen, Christie's, French & Co., American Art Association, Parke-Bernet, and Anderson Galleries.

Hearst's enthusiastic embrace of collecting and his voluminous purchases are well documented. The collections at San Simeon of antiquities, textiles, paintings, nineteenth-century sculpture, and ceilings reveal his expertise.

This work of art, entitled Bacchante, *is by American sculptor Frederick MacMonnies. The original bronze is in the Metropolitan Museum of Art in New York; this marble rendering was purchased by Phoebe Hearst.*

A red-figured Apulian pelike, or two-handled jar, used in the Greek colonies of southern Italy. It dates from the 5th century B.C.

This third-century Roman marble sarcophagus, located on the esplanade near "B" House, depicts the deceased as Apollo, accompanied by the Nine Muses. From left: Polyhymnia, Terpsichore, Thalia, Melpomene, Euterpe, Apollo, Athena, Clio, Erato, Urania, and Calliope.

Antiquities

Antiquities and classical subjects abound in virtually every medium at Hearst Castle. The most splendid collection at San Simeon is the Greek vases, which range from the early eighth century to the end of the fourth century B.C., and illustrate Greek figure painting at its finest. Metropolitan Museum of Art curator Dietrich von Bothmer notes that Greek vases were "prized from the moment they left the kiln," and praises eighty pieces the Metropolitan purchased from W.R. Hearst's estate. Hearst's interest in Greek vases was kindled in 1901 by his mother Phoebe. For the next fifty years Hearst added to this collection, making most of his purchases in the 1920s and 1930s. There are 155 vases remaining at San Simeon.

Art historians also commend the nine Classical sarcophagi found in the gardens at the Castle. The sarcophagus was used by the Romans as a coffin for above-ground interment. Most sarcophagi were made of marble or limestone and adorned with elaborate carving and inscriptions. Perhaps the finest example at San Simeon is a third-century Roman marble sarcophagus depicting the deceased as Apollo, accompanied by the Nine Muses, located on the esplanade near "B" House.

W. R. Hearst's collection of textiles includes tapestries and religious vestments. *Neptune Creating the Horse,* (above) a seventeenth-century Flemish work crafted from a cartoon by artist Jacob Jordaens, now hangs in the Assembly Room. The seventeenth-century heraldic banner (inset), made of silk velvet, features flags of twenty-three Spanish cities and principalities embroidered along the edges.

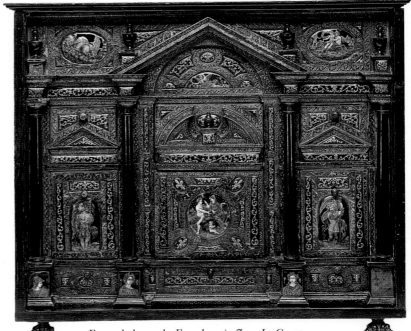

Enamel plaques by French artist Jean Le Court of Limoges enhance this sixteenth-centry jewel cabinet, located in the Billiard Room. The enamels depict scenes from the mythological life of Hercules.

Hearst's Gothic mille fleurs *tapestry hangs on the west wall of the Billiard Room. These tapestries derive their name from the carpet of flowers worked into the background. This rare example was probably completed in Flanders circa 1500.*

Textiles

San Simeon is also endowed with a magnificent collection of textiles, which Hearst bought to supplement those he had inherited from his mother. These textiles, including religious vestments, are used throughout *Casa Grande* and the guest houses as wall hangings and decorations.

The imposing Refectory, where Hearst and his guests dined, is dominated by the Palio banners suspended on staffs high above the room. Brightly-colored silk racing banners like these have been used since the thirteenth century at the biannual Palio Festival in Siena, Italy. Valued by collectors and art historians alike, the textiles were used to distinguish participants from various neighborhoods in Siena at the festivals. The Palio banners at Hearst Castle date to the eighteenth century, but are now too fragile for permanent display. The originals were removed by curators for conservation purposes and replaced with the painstakingly-made reproductions now seen on tour.

The earliest painting at San Simeon is located in Hearst's bedroom. Dating from the beginning of the fourteenth century, this striking Madonna and Child *was given to Hearst in 1932 by newspaper publisher Eleanor "Cissy" Patterson.*

W. R. Hearst's bedroom at San Simeon is surprisingly modest. The room is decorated with photographs and paintings of sentimental value, including pictures of his parents and maternal grandparents.

Perhaps the most notable of San Simeon's many textiles is the *mille fleurs* (literally "thousands of flowers") tapestry hanging in the Billiard Room. Woven of wool and silk, the tapestry depicts a stag hunt and was probably completed about 1500 in Flanders. One art expert believes it to be one of only "a handful of *mille fleurs* tapestries from this period in the entire world." It has been thoroughly examined by art experts on the Castle staff and by consultants from the Victoria and Albert Museum in London.

The tapestries on view in the massive Assembly Room illustrate an elaborate weaving style dating from the mid-sixteenth century. Four woven panels, each measuring over 300 square feet, depict the struggles of Roman general Scipio Africanus during the Punic Wars. The wool and silk Flemish

tapestries were made from drawings by Italian artist Giulio Romano and are considered rare as well as very beautiful.

Paintings

Most of the paintings at San Simeon were purchased by Hearst in the 1920s and early 1930s. One of the finest examples is Giulio Campi's *Portrait of a Woman*, hanging in a third-floor bedroom in the north wing of *Casa Grande*. The portrait, which Hearst acquired in London in 1929, dates from the early sixteenth century.

Throughout his life, Hearst was fascinated by Napoleon Bonaparte. He began collecting books and related materials at an early age, and would even dress as the conqueror at costume parties. In 1898, early in Hearst's career as a collector, he purchased two French oil paintings: *Bonaparte Before the*

Sphinx and *Bonaparte in Cairo*. The work of artist Jean-Léon Gérôme, a renowned and respected artist and sculptor, the paintings were completed in the late nineteenth century in the French salon style. The works now hang in the sitting room of the Celestial Suite.

Perhaps the most prized of Hearst's many paintings is the small but exquisite oil painting, *Madonna and Child*, from the School of Duccio di Buoninsegna. Located in Hearst's third-floor bedroom, the painting was given to him in 1932 by his friend and colleague, Eleanor "Cissy" Patterson, publisher of the Washington (D.C.) *Times-Herald*. Dating from the early fourteenth century, it is the earliest painting at San Simeon.

Giulio Campi's Portrait of a Woman *hangs in a third-floor bedroom in the north wing. The portrait dates from the early sixteenth century and was purchased by Hearst in London in 1929. Close examination of the painting reveals that the woman has a weasel on her lap, as well as a small dog.*

Some of the most prized guest rooms in Casa Grande were the four duplexes that Morgan designed. The south lower duplex, seen here, features two ceiling paintings by Simon Vouet depicting mythological scenes.

When at San Simeon, W. R. Hearst conducted business in his private enclave, the third-floor Gothic Library. Every day he retreated to this room with copies of Hearst papers flown in from distant cities. The papers were spread upon the floor, where, as one executive remembers, Hearst began a "sort of tap dance around and between them. It was a mild, uncostumed combination of Carmen Miranda, a rumba, a Russian dagger dance, and the Notre Dame shift, with lively castanet accompaniments produced by his snapping fingers. After I had observed W. R.'s strange dance, I learned it was his customary method of absorbing pictures and productions on his newspaper pages."

Bonaparte Before the Sphinx, *the work of artist Jean-Léon Gérôme, was one of Hearst's purchases as a young adult. Now on view in the Celestial Suite sitting room, this painting is accompanied by another Gérôme painting, entitled* Bonaparte in Cairo.

The east end of Hearst's private library is dominated by a portrait of the publisher at age 30, painted by his childhood friend, Orrin Peck.

The north bedroom in Casa Grande's *Gothic Suite displays a fifteenth-century Spanish ceiling with geometric shapes showing the Islamic influence in southern Spain. This room also contains seven Italian Renaissance panel paintings depicting the Madonna and Child.*

Sculpture

Two of San Simeon's finest statues, each executed in the highly Romantic style of the late nineteenth century, are found in the foyer of the Assembly Room. The first, entitled *Bacchante*, is a marble rendering of a work in bronze by American sculptor Frederick MacMonnies, who had a studio in Paris. The bronze sculpture, a dancing female nude with a baby in one hand and grapes held high in the other, was offered to the Boston Public Library by its original owner, architect Charles McKim. Boston's leading citizens protested the donation, arguing that the "work was improper for a building with intellectual purpose," because it glorified drunkeness, illegitimate motherhood, nudity, and a host of other immoralities. Hearst inherited MacMonnies's marble version of the sculpture from his mother.

The second statue is Jean-Léon Gérôme's *Pygmalion and Galatea*, another example of the Romantic style of the late Victorian period. The graceful rendering of the two figures is accomplished in white marble faintly tinted with paint. The theme of the sculpture is well known: the sculptor Pygmalion creates a female statue so beautiful he is unable to resist falling in love with it. Venus answers his prayers and brings the statue to life, naming her Galatea. Gérôme was one of Hearst's favorite artists; a fourth work by Gérôme at San Simeon is the bronze group, *Anacreon*, located in one of the duplex rooms in *Casa Grande*.

Ceilings

Rare antique ceilings are evident throughout the houses, often supplemented by plaster reproductions made by Morgan's craftsmen. Most of the historic ceilings are Spanish, acquired for Hearst by Arthur and Mildred Stapley Byne, art dealers who were once curators at the Hispanic Society of America in New York.

The painted pine ceiling with exposed beams that graces the Billiard Room is an excellent example of craftsmanship from northern Spain. It was offered to Hearst by art dealer Arthur Byne in 1930. Byne wrote to recommend the purchase, noting that the ceiling "is a very important fifteenth-century example, Gothic in period and style and similar to the one

The lobby of "A" House features this ceiling pendant. Crafted from gilded wood, it depicts the coat of arms and mitre of a sixteenth-century Spanish bishop.

Red velvet provides a striking contrast to the gilded sitting room of "A" House. Hearst acquired the painted trefoil arch over the picture window depicting the Crucifixion from French and Company in 1920.

The Doge's Suite sitting room is hung with many yards of blue brocade from Scalamandre, a famous New York textile firm.

recently put up in the Metropolitan Museum, New York. This ceiling is decorated in the best tradition of the Spanish ceiling painters, with the Moorish triangles formed of little white lozenges framing heraldic scenes. If you are not interested in it, I shall probably send it on to the Boston Museum." Hearst, of course, could not resist.

In Hearst's bedroom, Morgan installed a choice fourteenth-century Spanish ceiling. Exceedingly rare, the ceiling had long been separated from its frieze panels. Arthur Byne first found the ceiling in a house in the town of Tereul; he then found the original frieze panels in a nobleman's house in Aragon. Byne reunited the elements and offered the prized ceiling to Hearst, who had it shipped to San Simeon in 1924.

Italian sculptor Antonio Canova created this early nineteenth-century neoclassical rendering of Venus Emerging from the Bath. *Once owned by Lucien Bonaparte, the statue was acquired by Hearst from the Marquis of Lansdowne.*

Hearst's private Gothic sitting room, on the third floor, is dominated by ecclesiastical paintings and polychrome sculptures of saints.

San Simeon's movie theatre, lined with scarlet damask and supported by gilded caryatids, was used each evening to screen a new Hollywood film—often before it was released to the public.

A guest bathroom in the New Wing features black and white marble with brass fixtures.

One of two Celestial Suite bedrooms, located high above the main terrace in Casa Grande's towers.

Art deco pieces are seen in many rooms at San Simeon. This bronze and ivory sculpture by Gerdago was used to create a lamp.

Ceramic busts of two Renaissance noblemen are displayed in the lobby outside the Main Library.

All meals at San Simeon were prepared in Casa Grande's spacious kitchen. Food warmers in the middle of the room are surrounded by cupboards filled with liqueurs, china, stemware, and silver. Decorative kitchen fixtures and handmade tile (inset) were designed by Julia Morgan.

One of the bedrooms in "C" House features Persian pottery and a hanging silk Keshan rug.

Conserving San Simeon's Art Treasures

All museums have a dual mission—preservation and interpretation. Hearst Castle's art collection requires the care of conservators who restore and preserve art works as authentically as possible. For example, a conservator restoring an oil painting would add background only after applying an isolating layer between original paint and modern fills. Restored portions of a stone piece might be made visibly different to distinguish original from replaced materials. Fragile textiles may be supported by the addition of fine netting or a solid framework. Some extremely fragile art works are carefully reproduced, like the silk Palio banners in *Casa Grande*'s Refectory.

Stabilization and restoration of art is a painstaking job, necessary to preserve art for future generations. Conservators at Hearst Castle and other museums always treat each object as an individual piece with a history of its own.

A crew from the Office of the State Architect (OSA) handles the structural restoration vital to the buildings, terraces, and walkways at San Simeon. Here Casa Grande's *north tower is in scaffolding for restoration work on the cast stone architectural details.*

A staff member meticulously cleans the teak wood frieze on Casa Grande.

Artist Simon Vouet (1590-1649) was renowned for the ceiling paintings he created for the French court from 1627 through 1645. One of the duplex bedrooms contains this Vouet ceiling panel, entitled Neptune and Amphitrite.

An art conservator works on an oil-on-canvas panel in the lobby of "B" House (above). The paintings in the frieze were cleaned and stabilized, and "losses" were inpainted (right).

A curatorial staff member works under the direction of the curator, reproducing a Sienese Palio banner for display in the Refectory. Work on this eighteenth-century piece was completed in the conservation lab, open to public view in the Hearst Castle Visitor Center.

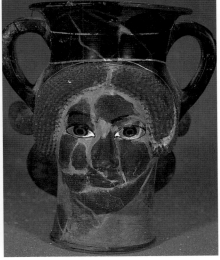

This Attic kantharos (left), or Greek cup, dates from the 5th century B. C. During conservation, photos using ultraviolet light (right) were made to detect earlier restoration that could not be seen in normal light.

Chapter Three

Life At The Castle

William Randolph Hearst's eminence as a film producer, coupled with the power of his vast newspaper and magazine holdings, made him an influential member of Hollywood society. San Simeon, although located over two hundred miles north of Hollywood's studios, beckoned to members of the film colony eager to advance their careers. Those who received the irresistible invitations for a weekend or more at San Simeon were drawn from a wide circle of friends, family, Hearst Corporation executives, business associates, politicians, journalists, celebrities, and athletes, as well as directors, writers, producers and stars in the motion picture industry.

The list of San Simeon guests is a virtual roll call of influential twentieth century figures, including aviators Charles Lindbergh and Amelia Earhart; the Duke and Duchess of Windsor; tennis stars Bill Tilden and Alice Marble; Hollywood producers and moguls Irving Thalberg, Louis B. Mayer, Harry Rapf, Paul Bern, and the Warner Brothers; political figures Fiorello Laguardia, Jimmy Walker,

Calvin and Grace Coolidge, and Winston Churchill; writers George Bernard Shaw, Aldous Huxley, and H.G. Wells; screenwriters Frances Marion, Herman Mankiewicz, and Charles Lederer; and movie stars Greta Garbo, John Gilbert, Jean Harlow, William Powell, Gloria Swanson, Marie Dressler, Buster Keaton, Leslie Howard, Cary Grant, Clark Gable, Carole Lombard, Mary Astor, Loretta Young, Delores del Rio, Charlie Chaplin, James Stewart, Joel McCrea, Joan Crawford, Douglas Fairbanks, Jr., and David Niven.

Those without a coveted invitation to the estate could only read about San Simeon in the popular press. A writer for *Fortune* in 1931 noted:

At the base of this hill you passed the airfield on which may land late Hearst newspapers from [distant] cities .... Continue on up the road, through what will be Sequoia forests a thousand-odd years from now, then give it one last swing and end it .... Standing there, you can look back, out over the hills to the Pacific; then look around you to find Moorish palaces amid enchanted gardens .... set off by the great twin towers of the Spanish mission cathedral which is La Casa Grande. You are now in the heart of the Hearst estate.

San Simeon guests dined in the Refectory, a vast dining hall hung with vivid racing banners and lined with silver pieces from Hearst's striking collection. (Inset) Detail of a doorway at the back courtyard of "C" House, decorated with Persian tile.

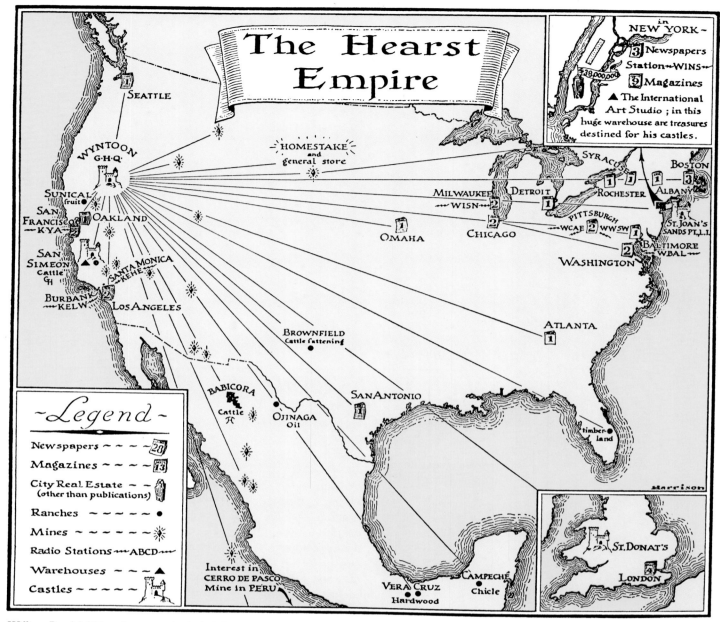

The Hearst Empire

SEATTLE

WYNTOON
G·H·Q·

SUNICAL fruit

SAN FRANCISCO
KYA

OAKLAND

SAN SIMEON
Cattle
G·H

SANTA MONICA
KEHE

BURBANK
KELW

LOS ANGELES

HOMESTAKE
and
general store

BROWNFIELD
Cattle fattening

BABICORA
Cattle

OJINAGA
Oil

SAN ANTONIO

MILWAUKEE
WISN

DETROIT

OMAHA

CHICAGO

WASHINGTON

PITTSBURGH
WCAE WWSW

SYRACUSE

ROCHESTER

ALBANY

BOSTON

ST. JOAN'S
SANDS PT., L.I.

BALTIMORE
WBAL

ATLANTA

timber-
land

VERA CRUZ
Hardwood

CAMPECHÉ
Chicle

Interest in
CERRO DE PASCO
Mine in PERU

in NEW YORK –
3 Newspapers
Station→WINS
9 Magazines
▲ The International
Art Studio ; in this
huge warehouse are treasures
destined for his castles.
$28,000,000

~Legend~

Newspapers ~ ~ ~ ~ — 20
Magazines ~ ~ ~ ~ — 13
City Real Estate ~ ~
(other than publications)
Ranches ~ ~ ~ ~ ~ — ●
Mines ~ ~ ~ ~ ~ — ✦
Radio Stations ~ ABCD
Warehouses ~ ~ ~ ▲
Castles ~ ~ ~ ~ 🏰

ST. DONAT'S

LONDON
4

Harrison

William Randolph Hearst's vast empire included newspapers, magazines, radio stations, ranches in the United States and Mexico, castles in America and Wales, and, of course, warehouses in a number of cities holding portions of his immense art collection.

Given Hearst's influence in the motion picture industry and the preponderance of San Simeon guests who worked within it, the ritual of screening films before their premiere was quickly established. Hearst reporter Adela Rogers St. Johns remembers:

> There was a motion picture run every single night come hell or high water . . . and to this every guest whether exalted or unimportant had to go. And stay. This was, I think, partly because Mr. Hearst loved movies and partly because he had a sort of paternal care for his high-spirited and temperamental guests and thought it might be dangerous for them to wander about at night, alone or in couples. (It often was.)

Actor Ralph Bellamy has several vivid memories of a mid–1930s visit he made to San Simeon. Before dinner, the guests had gathered in the Assembly Room, which Bellamy believes

> was quite accurately reproduced in Citizen Kane. Cocktails were being served at one end of the room and there was a chess game at the other end of the room. And I wandered over to the chess game and with the cocktails being served and a gramophone going, and though the limit was supposed to be one drink per person, there, some way or another, were more than that. The party was quite gay. But at the other end of the room at the chess game you could hardly hear over this commotion going on at the cocktail party.
>
> And in the midst of it, Mr. Hearst came [into the room.] There was a [teletype machine] just inside his right as

Whether reviewing his newspapers or conferring with his architect and art dealers, W. R. Hearst was never far from a telephone.

W. R. Hearst's estate at San Simeon, situated on a crest of the Santa Lucia mountains overlooking the sea.

Scores of Hollywood's famous actors, writers, directors, and producers gathered for convivial weekends at San Simeon. Back row, left to right: King Vidor, Beatrice Lillie, Richard Barthelmess, Eleanor Boardman. Middle row standing: Frank Orsatti, E.B. Hatrick, Edmund Goulding, "Ma" Talmadge, Greta Garbo, Nick Schenck, Alice Terry, Harry Rapf, Aileen Pringle, J. Robert Rubin, Norma Shearer. Seated: Hal Roach, Natalie Talmadge, Eddie Mannix, Constance Talmadge, Buster Keaton, Paul Bern, Irving Thalberg. Reclining: John Gilbert.

"The Flying San Simeons" (left) including Cary Grant (third from right) and Randolph Scott (second from right) performed acrobatics at a costume party with a circus theme hosted by W. R. Hearst. (Above) Newspaper publisher Eleanor "Cissy" Patterson, Hearst, and Marion Davies pose at a San Simeon party in the Refectory.

The Roman Pool was used by guests in the evenings. Every surface of the pool, walls, and ceiling are a mosaic of hammered gold and delicate Venetian glass tiles.

he came into the room and he stopped and he read it . . . . [Then] he went to a great enormous table in the center of the room and picked up a phone. I watched all this and listened to it. It was a direct connection with the San Francisco newspaper office and he asked for the editor and he said, "Put this in a two-column box on the front pages of all the papers tomorrow morning." And without notes, he dictated an editorial which appeared the following morning on the front page. . .

It was quite a remarkable thing to witness a man digesting the news, forming an opinion, creating a statement, and delivering it quite fluidly and with great ease, and its appearing the next day in a two-column box on the front page of all the papers.

Actor Joel McCrea recalled one mid-1930s weekend spent at San Simeon with his wife, actress Frances Dee; Gary Cooper; and his wife, socialite Veronica "Rocky" Balfe. At lunch it was announced that an impromptu costume party was planned that evening. "Coop and I looked at each other and said, 'We haven't got any [other clothes], except what we've got on.' And Mr. Hearst said, 'Don't worry about that. Go down and look.' He had about half the M-G-M wardrobe department! You could go as a fireman, a policeman, a sheik, Red

Cross nurse, whatever." McCrea and Cooper then attended the party as cowboys.

The social life at San Simeon thrived amid the constant din of construction. But early in 1937 Hearst's personal and business finances were precarious. Hearst's unrestrained buying sprees, the advent of Roosevelt's New Deal, and a sharp rise in taxes on personal wealth and large corporations, all contributed to his financial woes. Construction on the hilltop was restricted and sales were arranged for many of his art and book collections, some still in storage. Appraisers determined that Hearst collected 504 kinds of art, 20 of which

were outstanding. Hearst's accumulation of English silver and furniture, armor, tapestries, and Hispano-Moresque pottery were ranked among the finest private collections in the world. His financial position improved greatly when the government purchased a large tract of land from Hearst's San Simeon acreage for Fort Hunter-Liggett, an army installation.

The advent of World War II meant a sharp increase in newspaper sales, which strengthened Hearst's financial position. During the war, Hearst spent a great deal of his time at Wyntoon because it was believed that San Simeon was vulnerable to Japanese attack. After the war he returned to San Simeon, but in 1947 a heart attack forced him to leave the estate for the last time. He retreated to a relatively modest Beverly Hills estate at 1007 Lexington Drive to be close to cardiac specialists.

On August 14, 1951, William Randolph Hearst died at the age of 88, from a stroke complicated by "ailments of advanced age." His widow and five sons gathered in San Francisco for the funeral and the interment in the family mausoleum at Cypress Lawn Cemetery in Colma, California. His will, at 125 pages, was the longest ever filed in California and is sealed from the public. A portion of the estate, believed to total nearly $220 million, was left in trust to his family; the remainder was bequeathed to the California Charities (now the Hearst Foundation) as a charitable trust. Architect Julia Morgan died six years after Hearst at her home in San Francisco.

Construction at *La Cuesta Encantada* had stopped forever. Hearst's seaside estate is well-named for the pleasure it has given, first to William Randolph Hearst, his family and guests, and now to visitors from far and wide. San Simeon stands today as a lasting and unique tribute to the collaboration of architect Julia Morgan and her best-known client, William Randolph Hearst.

The impressive Refectory, (above) hung with Palio banners and lined with silver, was the site of many dinner parties. Hearst invited some of the era's most important and influential people to gather here. (Right) Hearst sometimes summoned his guests with a dinner bell from the main entrance of Casa Grande.

The entryway into the Assembly Room is flanked by Spanish baroque gilded wood columns and two fifteenth-century Venetian diptychs of Church fathers.

An aerial view of "The Enchanted Hill."

At left, a doe-eyed Marion Davies poses on a tapestry settee for an M-G-M studio photographer. She models a summer frock and cloche (above) on the esplanade in front of "A" House.

The sitting room in "C" House shows Hearst's strong interest in Spanish and Islamic art objects. Twelfth- through fourteenth-century Persian vases, Mudejar traveling chests and furniture, and two sixteenth-century portraits of Spanish royal family members decorate this room.

A statue of The Three Graces, *located across from the courtyard entrance to "A" House, is a favorite of San Simeon visitors.*

Hearst sometimes used historical novels as a basis for films featuring Marion Davies. Cosmopolitan Productions' silent epic, When Knighthood was in Flower *(1922) was a critical and commercial success. Always searching for new ways to promote his star, Hearst released "Marion Davies Editions" of the novels, now highly prized by collectors.*

Herds of zebra, descended from those in Hearst's private zoo, still roam the hills of the San Simeon ranch.

Domestic staff member Emma Christenson feeds a baby giraffe at San Simeon in the 1930s.

Camille Rossi, a foreman at San Simeon, shows off a trio of lion cubs from the San Simeon zoo.

Moonrise over San Simeon.

Guests were urged to accompany Hearst on lengthy horseback excursions over his 250,000-acre ranch. Marion Davies, who loathed trips on horseback, often jested that she would meet the riding party at their destination—in a limousine.

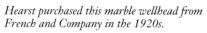

Hearst purchased this marble wellhead from French and Company in the 1920s.

Hearst was an early activist for animal rights. His beloved dog Helen sits on his lap in this photo. Helen enjoyed swimming with her master in the outdoor pool, and had a special place in the front row of the movie theater.

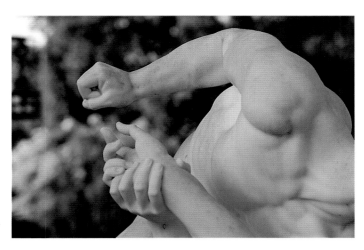

Dusk on "The Enchanted Hill," as seen from the Neptune Pool. (Left) Detail of The Wrestlers, *a copy of a Roman sculpture in the Uffizi Galley in Florence.*

Hearst San Simeon State Historical Monument

In 1957 the Hearst Corporation transferred ownership of renowned publisher and art collector William Randolph Hearst's San Simeon estate to the State of California for the dual purpose of historic interpretation and preservation. The State of California's Department of Parks and Recreation (formerly the Division of Parks and Beaches) has managed the Monument since that year, and opened "Hearst Castle" to the public for the first time on June 2, 1958. From the very first day demand for tours exceeded all projected estimates. By October 13, 1960, tour reservations were made available on a permanent basis. Within three years after its public opening, the Monument's annual visitor count rose to 312,000. By September of 1961 Hearst San Simeon State Historical Monument had logged its millionth visitor.

A dedicated staff of tour guides interpret San Simeon's grounds and buildings as an historic site for visitors. The Monument's permanent staff of trained professionals—including curators, preservation technicians, a historian, registrar, and photographer—catalog, preserve, and interpret the Castle's art and architecture. Restoration of art works is customarily performed by outside consultants under the direction of the chief curator.

San Simeon's Visitor Center, opened in 1987, houses permanent exhibits on the life and times of William Randolph Hearst, and on the construction of the estate Hearst usually referred to as "the Ranch." Additional displays introduce visitors to the beautiful landscape and other attractions of California's Central Coast. An observation area allows visitors to watch art conservators, preservation technicians and curatorial staff as they restore various *objets d'art* from the San Simeon collections. A ticket office, gift shop, and food and beverage service are also located in the complex.

Tours of Hearst Castle begin with a five-mile bus ride from the Visitor Center to the hilltop estate—the same route Hearst and his guests travelled. During the ride, exotic animals from Hearst's private zoo, including zebras, tahr goats, aoudad sheep, and fallow deer, might be seen. At the top of the hill, guides lead visitors on one of several walking tours through the Castle. Tour One, recommended for first-time visitors, provides an excellent introduction to the world that William Randolph Hearst and Julia Morgan created upon "The Enchanted Hill."

For additional information, contact:

Hearst San Simeon State Historical Monument
750 Hearst Castle Road
San Simeon, CA 93452-9741

The vista from San Simeon's hilltop.

Tours of Hearst Castle embark from San Simeon's Visitor Center, which includes a ticket office, historical exhibits, a conservation area, gift shop, and food and beverage service.